LEARN TO PLAY THE
DRUM SET

by PETER MAGADINI

This book is dedicated in memory of Carl Elmer.

Back cover photo by: Joyce Woo

INTRODUCTION

Perhaps you're a young aspiring newcomer to music, or maybe an experienced musician whose passion for the drums has finally pushed you into purchasing a complete drum set. Whatever the reason for your decision to study the drums, you've chosen an instrument that is extremely versatile and one that is heard almost daily by anyone exposed to music. Drums and drummers have been around since man first hit a log with a stick and the art of playing the instrument has expanded and matured to a level that makes drums one of the most popular instruments in the world.

This book was written to teach you the basics of the drum set in the shortest amount of time and will explain how the drum set functions in many styles of contemporary music. In addition to learning the basics of reading and improvisation, you'll also learn the coordination of hands and feet...all in a practical but fun-filled manner. So, if you're learning on your own or with the help of a teacher, the results will be an exciting and rewarding musical experience.

CONTENTS

HAL•LEONARD®
CORPORATION

7777 W. BLUEMOUND RD. P.O. BOX 13819 MILWAUKEE, WI 53213

THE DRUM SET

For many years, the basic drum set consisted of four drums...the bass drum; the tenor tom-tom (or high tom-tom); the floor tom-tom (or low tom-tom); and the snare drum.

BASIC FOUR PIECE SETUP

snare drum

tenor tom-tom

bass drum

floor tom-tom

More recently, many drum authorities (myself included) consider an added tenor tom-tom mounted on the other side of the bass drum as a contemporary basic set-up.

Many drums (including an additional bass drum) can be added to a basic set-up. However, it's my opinion that adding drums at a later stage of development is much less of a problem once you learn to master various techniques on a basic set-up. Therefore, I've designed the contents of this book to generally apply to either the basic four piece or basic five piece drum set.

BASIC FIVE PIECE SETUP

crash cymbal

ride cymbal

hi-hat cymbals

two tenor tom-toms

TUNING (TENSIONING) THE DRUM SET

Drums are not actually tuned to a specific pitch. If they were, they'd have to be retuned with each different piece or even every change of chord. They are tuned (some drummers prefer the term tensioned) so that the drums being played range from higher to lower without emphasis being placed on actual pitches.

The following **instructions** explain how to tune the bass drum. The same procedure should be followed for all the other drums. Keep in mind that the tom-toms are tensioned so they sound from high to low as you move from left to right while playing. The snare drum, as a rule is tensioned tighter than the bass drum and the tom-toms.

Clockwise, work your way around the drum turning each tuning rod a few times. Do this until the head becomes evenly tensioned all the way around (there should be no ripples anywhere on the surface).

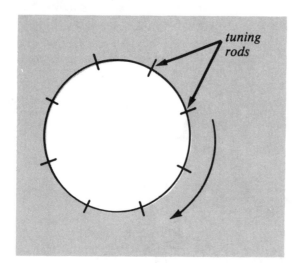

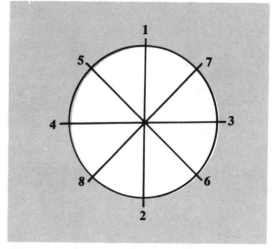

You may also gain the same results by criss-cross tuning.

When the head is sufficiently tight, take one hand and put it palm down in the middle of the drum head. Place the other hand on top and press firmly on the head with both hands. Do not be disturbed if you hear a cracking or popping sound. This is merely the new head adjusting itself to the added tension. Once this is done, the head will hold the tension consistently wherever you set it. This is called **seating the head**. As stated previously, **the same procedure should be followed on all drum heads**.

ARRANGING YOUR SET

Now that you've tuned your drums, it will be necessary to set them up so that you can achieve the maximum results with the minimum amount of motion. Since no two drummers are the same shape or size, here are some simple suggestions to follow:

1 Adjust your seat so that your legs are straight out from your hips and are parallel to the floor. Your knees should be bent at approximately a 90° angle and your feet should feel comfortable on the pedals. (Your left foot should be on the hi-hat pedal and your right foot on the bass drum foot pedal.)

2 The snare drum should be directly in front of you and approximately belt buckle high.

3 The tenor tom-tom should be above and to the left of the snare drum. It should be tilted downward toward the snare drum at a 40° angle.

NOTE: If two tenor tom-toms are used, the second one should also tilt toward the snare drum.

4 The floor tom should be placed as close as possible to your bass drum leg and just a bit lower than the height of the snare drum.

5 The hi-hat cymbals should be set 6 to 10 inches higher than the snare drum. The space between the hi-hat cymbals should be approximately 1/2 to 1 inch.

6 The stands which hold the ride cymbal and crash cymbal should be placed as closely to the set as possible and approximately 6 to 12 inches above the tenor tom-toms. The cymbals should tilt a bit toward the snare drum head. They must be close enough to reach with ease but not so close that they interfere with the sticks as you maneuver around the set.

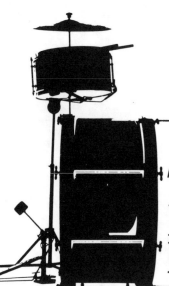

THE PRACTICE PAD

The practice pad and the practice pad set are logical substitutes for the real thing. In many cases, practice on the live set is impractical or impossible due to the close proximity of neighbors and family. Therefore, a practice pad set may be a necessary practicing tool depending upon your own personal situation.

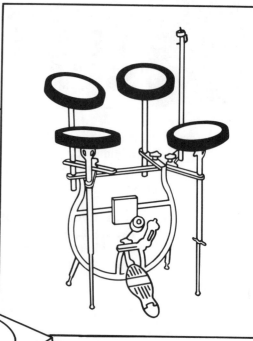

Practice Pad Set

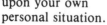

←**Practice Pad**

THE DRUMSTICK

The drumstick is your tool. Without it, drum set playing as we know it would be impossible. If possible, I suggest you get some professional help in picking out the proper drumsticks for your hand. If no professional help is available, try to find drumsticks of a medium weight. Roll the sticks on the countertop to make sure they are not warped. A straight stick is an absolute requirement for maximum playing results.

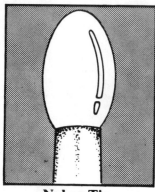

Nylon Tip

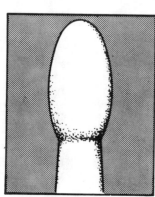

Wood Tip

HOLDING THE STICKS

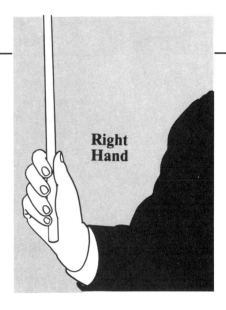

Right Hand

The first decision you have to make as a new drummer is which grip to use to hold the sticks. There are two...the Conventional grip (also called the over and under grip) and the Matched grip. Following is an explanation of both.

The Conventional Grip

In this grip the right hand **(the opposite if you're left handed)** is held with the thumb and index finger holding the stick just behind the lettering which appears on it. Think of a pin going through the thumb, stick, and index finger in a straight line and the stick pivoting at that point. The other fingers **all** gently rest **on** the stick and follow the motion of the drumstick. With the Conventional grip the right hand moves from the wrist in an up and down motion.

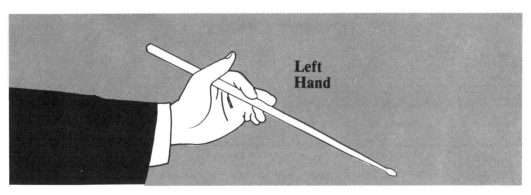

Left Hand

With the left hand, the stick is held at the point where the thumb and index finger join the hand. The top two fingers (index and middle) rest over the top of the stick while the remaining two fingers are under the stick. The thumb is positioned over the stick and gently rests on the index finger. With the Conventional grip the left wrist moves much the same as when you turn a doorknob.

The Matched Grip

The other popular grip is the **matched grip.** With this grip, both hands are held like the right hand grip (described in the **conventional grip** copy). There are two distinct advantages to the matched grip: (1) both hands are held exactly the same and require only one wrist motion; (2) many drummers find it easier to maneuver around the drum set.

Matched Grip

Try both grips. Choose the one that seems to fit you the best.

STARTING TO PLAY

Sit comfortably at the drum set. Hold your sticks in the Matched grip or Conventional grip position. Then let your arms drop to your sides with the sticks resting loosely in your hands. Next, bring your arms up from the elbow so that they are at a 90° angle to your body and are parallel to the floor. This is the proper playing position for the drum set. Notice that your shoulders and upper arms are in a completely relaxed position.

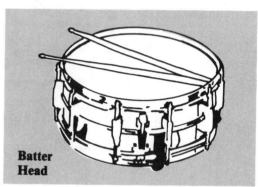
Batter Head

The first drum that you'll play on is the snare drum.

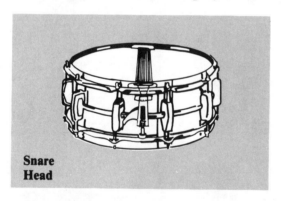
Snare Head

The top head of the snare drum is called the batter head. The bottom head is called the snare head. The tensioning procedure is the same as the bass drum. In order to arrive at a clean, clear snare drum sound, both heads should be tensioned tightly. The snares should contact the snare head evenly without being too loose. Snares that do not contact the head properly may result in unwanted buzzing of the snare drum when the other drums are being played.

Exercise for the hands:

1 Play four taps on the snare drum with the right hand.

2 Play four taps on the snare drum with the left hand.

 **Play four taps on the snare drum with each hand. Do this several times.**

NOTE:

If a deeper sound is required from the snare drum, leave the bottom head tensioned tightly but loosen the top head about 10 to 20 percent. While tuning, keep in mind that the head tension should be approximately the same at every tension screw.

The next drum you'll play on is the bass drum.

 **Exercise for the feet:** Play eight even strokes on the bass drum (use your right foot on the bass pedal). Do this several times.

The first cymbal we'll use is the hi-hat cymbal.

 The hi-hat cymbals are the two cymbals that are clamped to the hi-hat stand. Place your left foot on the pedal at the base of the hi-hat stand, and play eight even beats with the hi-hat.

(hi-hat exercise notation)

 Now, repeat the bass drum beats. Along with it, play the hi-hat on every other beat. Do this several times.

SOME BASIC MUSIC ELEMENTS

THE STAFF

Music is written on a structure called a staff. The staff consists of five horizontal lines and the four spaces between these lines. On melodic instruments, each line or space represents a specific pitch. Since drums do not normally play specific pitches, the various staff positions are used to represent different drums and cymbals. For example, the snare drum is represented by notes placed in the third space; the bass drum by notes written in the first space; the hi-hat cymbal by x's written directly below the first line.

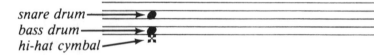

snare drum
bass drum
hi-hat cymbal

As new drums or cymbals are introduced, a new staff position will be used to show you the pattern that must be played on that drum or cymbal.

TIME VALUES

Divisions of time in music are called beats. The physical appearance of a note tells exactly how many beats it receives. The following illustration shows the most common types of notes and their time values.

WHOLE NOTE	HALF NOTE	QUARTER NOTE
4 beats	2 beats	1 beat

RESTS

Rests are symbols used in music to indicate a period of silence. The physical appearance of a rest determines how long the period of silence will be. The following illustration shows the most common rests and their corresponding time values.

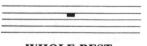  

WHOLE REST	HALF REST	QUARTER REST
4 beats of silence	2 beats of silence	1 beat of silence

BAR LINES AND MEASURES

Each staff is divided into sections by vertical lines called BAR LINES. The sections between bar lines are called MEASURES. A double bar line (‖) indicates the end of a song.

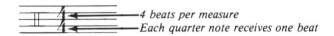

THE $\frac{4}{4}$ TIME SIGNATURE

From now on, at the beginning of each exercise or rhythm pattern in this book, there will be a set of two numbers called the TIME SIGNATURE. While there are many different time signatures, the one used in this book is $\frac{4}{4}$. The upper number tells how many beats there are in each measure, and the bottom number tells what kind of note receives one beat.

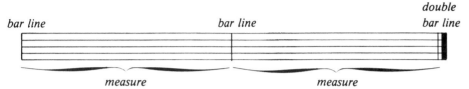

COUNTING AND THE SINGLE STROKE

The single stroke (or single stroke roll as it is sometimes referred to) is the rapid succession of single beats performed by alternating the hands so that the drum sticks strike the drum evenly from one stick to another.

Your hands should move from the wrists only, and the sticks should be held comfortably. It is important not to hold the stick too tightly so that the **natural** rebound of the drumstick can be utilized. To help you acquire speed and control of this important fundamental rudiment, exaggerate the motion of the wrists in order to follow the rebounding stick.

Repeat Signs

Repeat signs are used to indicate that a certain section of music is to be played again. Most often, repeat signs appear in sets of two. There is a repeat sign ‖: at the beginning of a section to be repeated and another repeat sign :‖ at the end of a section. When two repeat signs are present, play to the second repeat sign and then return to the first repeat sign and play the entire section once more.

Count quarter notes while playing the single stroke on the snare drum (or practice pad).

f *(Abbreviation for the Italian word **forte** which means to play loudly)*

Cont...

Eighth Notes

When a quarter note is divided in half, a new type of note called the eighth note is formed. Eighth notes are played twice as fast as quarter notes. Each eighth note (♪) or eighth rest (𝄾) is worth 1/2 beat.

Because it takes two eighth notes to equal one quarter, it is then possible to have eight eighth notes in each bar.

When playing eighth notes count as follows:

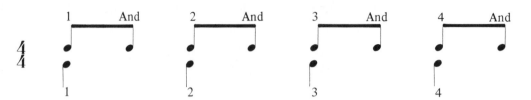

A single stroke exercise - The purpose of the following exercise is the development of control and speed of the single stroke. Begin the exercise slowly and gradually. Increase the speed of the hands until you're playing as fast as possible. Maintain the fastest speed for a few seconds, then reverse the procedure by **gradually** slowing down until you are back to the original tempo.

Be sure to rotate your hands with a maximum wrist turn in accordance with the natural rebound of the drumstick.

In the following exercise, the notes show **slow to fast to slow** only and should not be interpreted exactly as written.

SLOW   **FASTER**   **FAST**   **SLOWER**   **SLOW**

Notice that as the strokes get faster, the rebounds are closer to the drum head.

The following is a basic drum set pattern in quarter notes. The x's marked directly above the top line of the staff indicate the part played on the ride cymbal (for location of the ride cymbal see page 3).

A basic drum set pattern in quarter notes

Exercise Breakdown:

● **Play the bass drum**

● **Add the ride cymbal**

12

● **Add the hi-hat on counts 2 and 4**

Hi-Hat

● **Complete the pattern by adding the snare drum on counts 2 and 4 along with the hi-hat**

QUARTERS AND EIGHTHS

1 *Counting and playing quarter notes*

In order to play and read at the drum set it is important that you know how to stop and start the hands while the feet continue playing. Begin the following exercise on the bass drum by playing steady quarter notes in $\frac{4}{4}$ time. Then add the hi-hat on 2 & 4 as indicated by the x. After you have started your feet playing in a comfortable $\frac{4}{4}$ pattern, proceed to play the exercise. Alternate the right and left hands on the snare drum. Remember to keep the feet going, but do not play the snare drum on the rests.

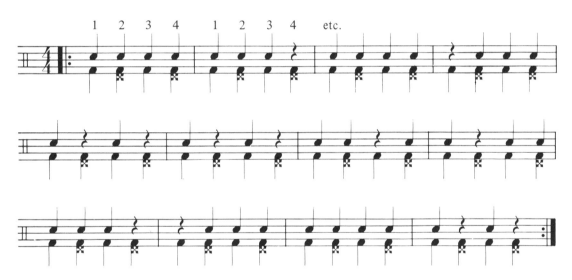

2 *Counting and playing eighth notes*

13

PLAYING AROUND THE SET

The following exercise uses three tom-toms. The notes written in the fourth space of the staff indicate the beats that must be played on tenor tom #1. The notes written in the third space indicate the beats that must be played on tenor tom #2. The notes written in the second space indicate the beats that must be played on the floor tom.

NOTE: The circled symbol (⊗) written above the staff indicates the crash cymbal.

Eighth Notes and Quarter Notes around the set

Play the quarter notes on the snare drum and tom-toms as written. Start each of the following exercises slowly. As the exercises become more familiar, increase the tempo.

> = *Accented Note: to be played louder than the other notes*

This exercise is designed for the basic five piece drum set (two tenor toms). If you have the four piece set (one tenor tom), double the tenor tom drum part on the one drum. If you have more than the basic five piece setup, choose the toms that will accommodate the exercise.

2 Now add the bass drum and hi-hat.

3 Play eighth notes around the set as written.

4 Now add the bass drum and hi-hat to the eighth note exercise.

EIGHTH NOTE PATTERNS ON THE DRUM SET

In this lesson you'll learn some modern eighth note patterns that can be applied to most eighth note based music. You will also learn to use independent bass drum technique against the basic pulse of the snare drum and ride cymbal pattern. You should practice playing the ride cymbal pattern both on the ride cymbal and on the closed hi-hat. When playing on the ride cymbal, the hi-hat closes as usual on 2 and 4. However, when playing on the closed hi-hat, keep the hi-hat cymbals closed tightly together throughout.

1 Rock pattern in $\frac{4}{4}$ time

Exercise Breakdown:

● **Play the bass drum**

● **Add the hi-hat on counts 2 and 4**

● **Add the ride cymbal in eighths (two eights to every one quarter)**

● **Add the snare drum along with the hi-hat on counts 2 and 4**

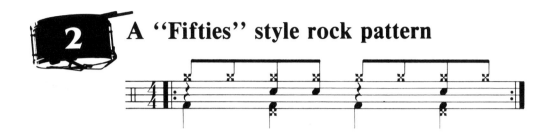

2 A "Fifties" style rock pattern

Exercise Breakdown

● **Play the ride cymbal in even eighths**

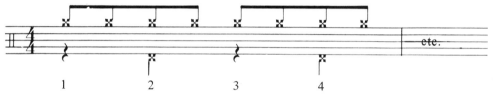

1 & 2 & 3 & 4 &

● **Add the hi-hat on counts 2 and 4 ·**

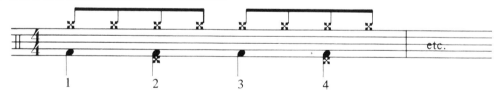

1 2 3 4

● **Add the bass drum on all 4 counts**

1 2 3 4

● **Add the snare drum on counts 2 and 4 (accent the snare drum but not the cymbals)**

3 Rock pattern with the bass drum in eighth notes

1 & 2 & 3 & 4

Exercise Breakdown

● **Play the ride cymbal in even eighths**

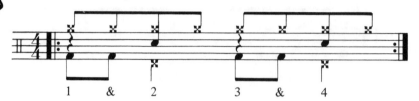

1 & 2 & 3 & 4 & etc.

● **Add the hi-hat on counts 2 and 4**

2   4   etc.

● **Add the bass drum part**

1 & 2 & 3 & 4   etc.

● **Add the snare drum on counts 2 and 4**

etc.

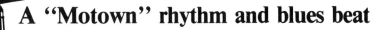

4 A "Motown" rhythm and blues beat

Exercise Breakdown

● **Play the ride cymbal in even eighths**

● **Add the hi-hat on counts 2 and 4**

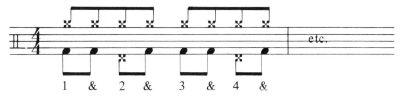

● **Add the bass drum part**

● **Add the snare drum on counts 2 and 4**

5 "Disco" beat

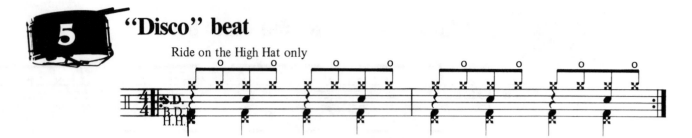

Ride on the High Hat only

Notice that both the bass drum and the hi-hat play on all 4 beats of the bar. The hi-hat ride beat is therefore a series of open (o) and closed eighth notes. This happens automatically when you play the eighths on the hi-hat as it opens and closes on the four quarter notes of the bar.

Exercise Breakdown

● **Play on the closed hi-hat even eighths**

● **With the hi-hat foot play quarter notes (continue the ride)**

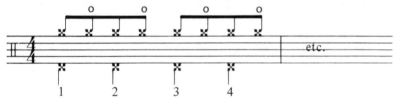

● **Add the bass drum**

● **Add the snare drum on counts 2 and 4**

6 Bass drum on the upbeats

Exercise Breakdown

● **Play the ride cymbal**

etc.

● **Add the hi-hat**

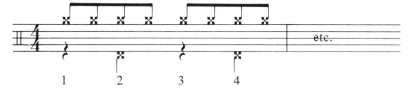

1   2   3   4

etc.

● **Add the bass drum**

1 & 2 & 3 & 4 &

etc.

● **Add the snare drum**

etc.

7 Improvise

Improvise your own bass drum eighth note patterns against the ride cymbal, hi-hat and snare drum.

8 Playing a drum fill*

Play the basic rock pattern for two bars. Go from bar (2) to bar (3) without stopping the time and play the drum "Fill" around the drum set in single strokes in bars 3, 4, 5 and 6. Notice the bass drum changes to quarter notes during the drum fill. After playing the written rock pattern, play the other previously learned patterns with this drum fill exercise.

Repeat to the beginning without stopping the time.

*A drum fill is a short drum solo used to add excitement to the band. Drum fills may be written out or improvised for a predetermined number of bars. The above drum fill is four bars long.

THE DOUBLE STROKE ROLL (bounce strokes)

(bounce strokes)
Example:

R R L L R R L L R R L L R R L L R R

Many professionals feel that the two most fundamental rudiments required for drum set playing are the single stroke and double stroke. Most of the other drum rudiments are combinations of these two.

When you begin playing the double stroke, start slowly by making two distinct taps with each hand. As you play faster, the second tap changes to a stick bounce. In order to do this, you strike the drum head once and then allow the natural rebound of the drumstick to make the second tap automatically. It's important to learn to control the natural rebound (bounce) of the drumstick.

 **1**   ## The double stroke — slow to fast to slow

Start slowly and gradually increase the speed of the double stroke until the sticks are rebounding comfortably in the hands; then, gradually return to the original tempo.

slow to fast - to slow

R R L L R R L L R R L L R R L L R R L L R R L L R R L L R R L L R R L L R R L L

no bounce - - - - - - - - - - - - to bounce - to no bounce

 2   ## The open roll

The roll is the drummer's way of sustaining sound from the drum.

The open roll is the double stroke played at a fast steady tempo. The important thing to remember about the **open** roll is that the drumsticks never play more than two taps in each hand, no matter how fast the roll is played.

Cont....

fast and steady

R R L L   R R L L   R R L L   etc.

Rolls as notated in drum music look like this.

Example:

1   2   3   4   1   2   3   4   1   2   3   4

The previous example means each whole note is rolled for the entire four count duration of each bar. The rhythm of the double strokes should be as fast as it takes to keep the roll tight. In other words the basic tempo of the quarter note does not dictate the speed of the hands.

SIXTEENTH NOTES

Counting and playing sixteenths

Sixteenth notes are the equivalent of the quarter note divided into four equal parts. Therefore, each sixteenth note gets 1/4 of a count.

Example:

Sixteenth notes are counted as follows:

1 E & A   2 E & A   3 E & A   4 E & A

1 **Count and play sixteenths on the snare drum.**

1 E & A 2 E & A 3 E & A 4 E & A   1   2 E & A 3   4 E & A

1 E & A 2 E & A 3   4 E & A   1 E & A 2   3 E & A 4

2 **Play the same exercise with the bass drum and hi-hat included.**

1 ## Sixteenths and the drum set
Play double strokes in sixteenth notes on the snare drum.

2 **Play the following exercise around the set.**

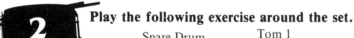

3 **Play the following exercise with single strokes.**

Improvising with Sixteenths *(using single and double strokes)*

Singles and doubles on the snare drum

- After mastering the preceding on the snare drum, play the same exercise around the drum set.

- Play the exercise as written. However, while you are playing, move from one drum to another. Play the exercise with a steady tempo and include your bass drum and hi-hat.

Improvise with double strokes in sixteenth notes around the set. Include the bass drum and hi-hat.

Example:

Keep the sixteenths flowing smoothly as you move from one drum to another.

Improvise with single strokes in sixteenth notes around the set. Include the bass drum and hi-hat.

Example:

1 EIGHTH AND SIXTEENTH COMBINATION STROKES ON THE SNARE DRUM

Play on the snare drum only with alternate sticking.

2 The previous exercise with the bass drum and hi-hat included.

3

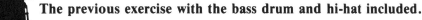

4 The previous exercise with the bass drum and hi-hat included.

5

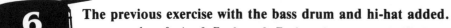

6 The previous exercise with the bass drum and hi-hat added.

SIXTEENTH AND EIGHTH NOTE ROCK PATTERNS

Eighths and sixteenths with the bass drum against the eighth note ride

1 A "Funk" pattern with sixteenth notes on the bass drum

Exercise Breakdown

● Play the ride cymbal

- **Add the hi-hat**

- **Add the bass drum**

- **Add the snare drum**

2 A "Funk" pattern with eighth note upbeats on the bass drum

Exercise Breakdown

- **Play the ride cymbal**

- **Add the hi-hat**

- **Add the bass drum**

- **Add the snare drum**

3 Double time sixteenth note pattern on the bass drum

*NOTE: A dot adds half the value to the note or rest that precedes it. Therefore, the rest in this example is the value of two sixteenths ($\mathcal{7}\mathcal{7}$) and the dot adds one more sixteenth ($\mathcal{7}\mathcal{7}\mathcal{.}$). The last sixteenth is written ($\mathcal{7}\mathcal{7}\mathcal{7}$).

Exercise Breakdown

● **Play the ride cymbal**

● **Add the hi-hat**

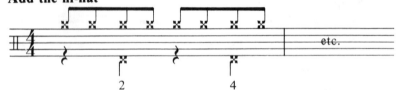

● **Add the bass drum**

● **Add the snare drum**

4 "Salsa" feel bass drum pattern

Exercise Breakdown

● **Play the ride cymbal**

● **Add the hi-hat**

● **Add the bass drum**

● **Add the snare drum**

5 Improvise your own bass drum patterns against the ride cymbal. The hi-hat may play on beats 2 and 4 or all 4 beats. The snare should continue on the 2 and 4 "back beat" pattern. NOTE: The ride cymbal part may also be played on the closed hi-hat.

6 **Play sixteenth notes on the ride cymbal or closed hi-hat and repeat exercises 1 through 4 on pages 28 through 31.**

A drum fill in sixteenth notes

7 Play and learn the exercise with the rock pattern that's written. Play the drum fill using both single strokes and double strokes. Experiment by substituting some of the other rock patterns in the first two bars of this exercise.

8 Repeat the drum fill exercise. However, this time use sixteenths on the ride cymbal. Play the drum fill as you did in exercise 7.

THE TRIPLET

A triplet is a group of three notes (indicated on the music by a number "3") which are played in the same amount of time ordinarily given two notes of the same time value.

For example:

The eighth note triplet divides the quarter note into three equal parts.

1   **Count and play triplets in 4/4 time on the snare drum.**

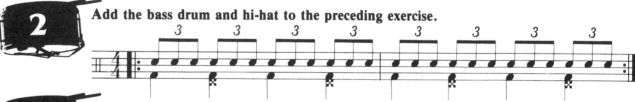

2   **Add the bass drum and hi-hat to the preceding exercise.**

3   **Count and play triplets around the set.**

4   **Add the bass drum and hi-hat to the above exercise.**

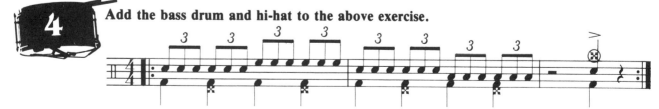

5   **Improvise around the set with triplets using single strokes only. Keep a steady beat with the bass drum and hi-hat.**

THE RIDE CYMBAL AND JAZZ (SWING)

The ride cymbal carries one of the most important functions of the drum set. That function is playing "the time" (keeping the beat), and establishing the rhythmic feel of the piece being played. The ride cymbal is the heart of the rhythm section. (The rhythm section in a band includes: drums, bass, keyboard, percussion and guitar.)

Earlier you played a basic rock pattern. Now you'll learn the basic jazz ride cymbal pattern.

The ride cymbal pattern comes from the triplet rhythm:

Example:

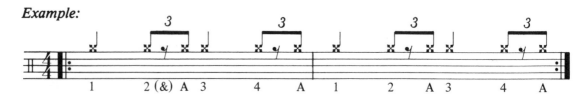

This pattern may also be shown as follows:

(The words "play today" fit the rhythm of the jazz ride cymbal pattern.)

The ride cymbal is played with one hand only. The right hand for right handed drummers and the left hand for left handed drummers.

The cymbal should be played with the bead of the stick near the edge of the cymbal.

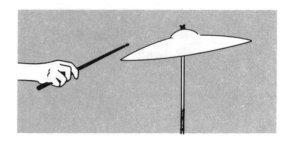

1 ## Basic drum set jazz swing pattern in $\frac{4}{4}$ time

34

Exercise Breakdown

- **Play the ride cymbal**

1   2   A   3   4   A   1   2   A   3   4   A

- **Add the bass drum**

1   2   3   4   1   2   3   4

- **Add the hi-hat on counts 2 and 4**

- **Add the snare drum along with the hi-hat on counts 2 and 4**

The jazz ride beat works with many styles of music including jazz, folk, country, swing, bluegrass and dixieland. Find some recordings that include one of these categories and listen for the ride cymbal. If possible, set your drum set up close to the speakers and play along. Headphones work the best.

Here is a diagram of the best way to set up while playing along with the radio or stereo.

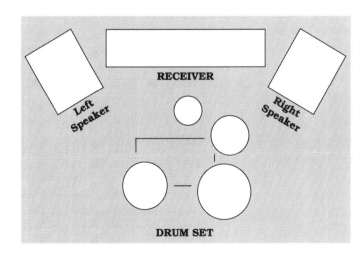

35

The Shuffle rhythm

The shuffle rhythm is the forerunner of the jazz ride cymbal beat and still is the basic rhythmic pattern for many blues compositions. It, too, is based on the triplet rhythm.

Example:

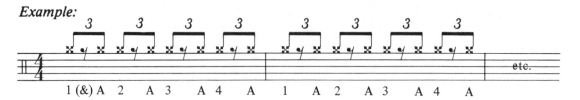

The shuffle rhythm may also be shown as follows:

"Kansas City" shuffle

NOTE: *When playing this shuffle beat, the ride cymbal and the snare drum are both accented.*

Exercise Breakdown

● **Play the ride cymbal**

● **Add the bass drum and hi-hat**

● **Add the snare drum along with the ride cymbal with an accent on counts 2 and 4**

INDEPENDENCE AND THE RIDE CYMBAL

The term independence refers to the technique of playing patterns on the snare drum that complement the music while the ride cymbal continues its pattern uninterrupted.

1 ## The jazz ride cymbal pattern and the shuffle rhythm played at the same time

Exercise Breakdown

● **Play the ride cymbal**

● **Add the bass drum and hi-hat**

● **Add the shuffle rhythm on the snare drum**

2 Jazz ride cymbal pattern and triplets played at the same time

Exercise Breakdown

● **Play the ride cymbal**

● **Add the bass drum and hi-hat**

● **Add the snare drum in triplets**

3 **Mixed patterns:**

There are endless combinations of patterns that may be played against the jazz cymbal ride. Eventually you will learn to play patterns with hands and feet independently, adding punctuation to the over-all rhythmic feel.

4 **Improvise your own independent patterns against the jazz cymbal ride pattern. Keep the ride cymbal and patterns musical and flowing.**

(Improvise your own snare drum patterns)   etc.

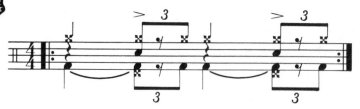

Country "two beat" swing pattern

Exercise Breakdown

● **Play the ride cymbal**

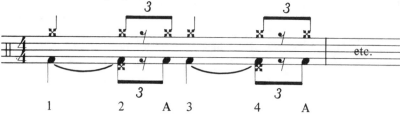

● **Add the hi-hat on counts 2 and 4**

● **Add the bass drum**
NOTE: *A tie is a curved line which connects notes on the same line or space of the staff. The value of the second note is added to the first note. The tied note is counted but* **not** *played.*

● **Add the snare drum on counts 2 and 4**
NOTE: Only the snare drum should be accented.

6 Nashville country rock

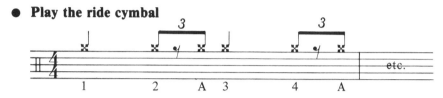

Exercise Breakdown

● **Play the ride cymbal**

● **Add the hi-hat**

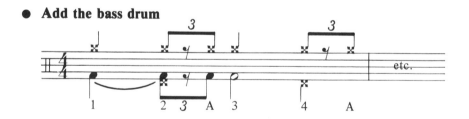

● **Add the bass drum**

● **Add the snare drum**

7 A drum fill in triplets

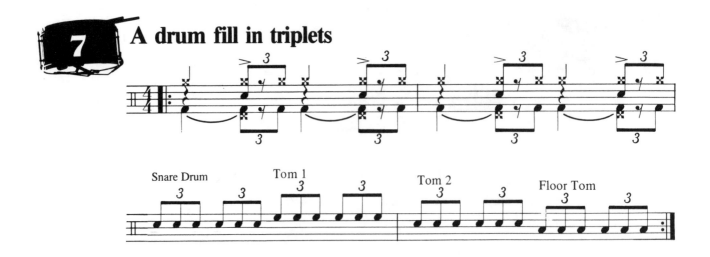

8 Slow blues beat

The next pattern has the abbreviation M.M. (Maelzel's Metronome) ♩ = 60 written at the beginning of the music. The Metronome is a mechanical device which helps to keep time by making a clicking sound a specified number of times per minute. This particular mark means that the Metronome should be set at 60 and each click represents the length of a quarter note. Metronome marks indicate tempo. If at first you cannot play the pattern at this tempo, practice it slower and gradually increase the speed as it becomes more comfortable.

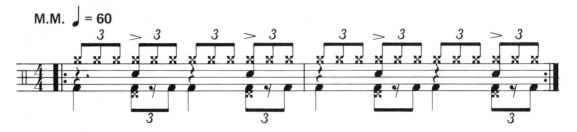

Exercise Breakdown

● **Play the ride cymbal**

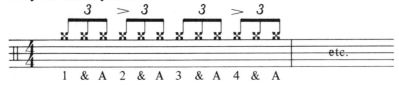

● **Add the hi-hat**

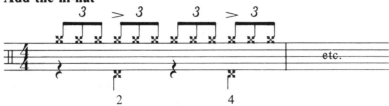

● **Add the bass drum**

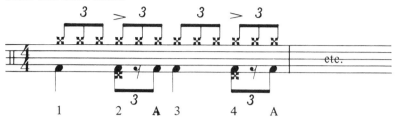

● **Add the snare drum**

9 Slow blues beat with a sixteenth note fill

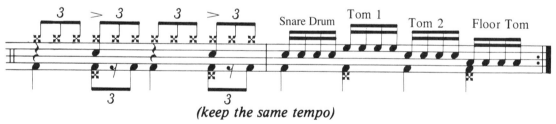

(keep the same tempo)

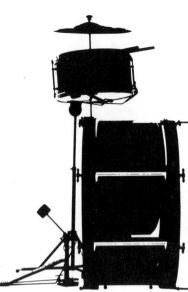

VALUABLE SNARE DRUM RUDIMENTS

Three valuable snare rudiments:

 ## The Flam

The flam beat requires concentration and dexterity in order to be played well. The flam is comprised of a main note preceded by a grace note. The grace note is played close to the main note and is considered part of the same beat.

Example:

The grace note indicates that the drum is struck first and the main note indicates that the drum is struck immediately after the grace note. The hand playing the grace note will always be closer to the drum head. When one flam is played, the hands then reverse so the hand that played the main note will now play the grace note. Always aim to keep the grace note hand still and close to the drum while you are switching hands for the next flam.

2 ## The Closed Roll or Buzz Roll

The closed roll, often referred to as the buzz or press roll, is a series of buzz sounds from each alternating stick. To begin developing the buzz roll, play a short relaxed buzz with each stick. After you can play a clear buzz in each hand, increase the speed until the "buzz" connects into one continuous sound.

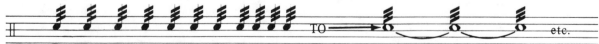

Closed Buzz Roll
p *(soft)*

44

Cont...

In order to play the buzz roll louder you must apply more pressure to the drumstick and at the same time increase the speed of the alternating hands.

$pp \qquad p \qquad mf \qquad f \qquad ff \qquad f \qquad mf \qquad p \qquad pp$

Practice playing the buzz roll from soft to loud to soft. Take your time.

The dynamic markings translate as follows:

pp — pianissimo	— very soft	**f** — forte	— loud
p — piano	— soft	**ff** — fortissimo	— very loud
mf — mezzoforte	— medium loud		

3 The five stroke roll

The five stroke roll may be played both open and closed and is comprised of three hand motions. The first two hand motions are bounce strokes while the third hand motion is a single tap. The five stroke roll alternates from hand to hand.

Exercise Breakdown

● **The open five stroke roll**

bounce bounce tap   bounce bounce tap

● **The closed five stroke roll**

buzz buzz tap   buzz buzz tap

● **Eighth notes and the five stroke roll (bass drum and hi-hat included)**

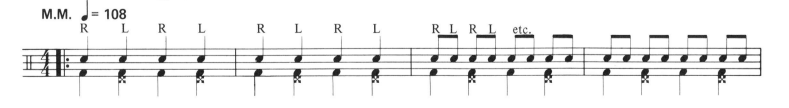

4 An exercise for the snare drum, bass drum and hi-hat

M.M. ♩ = 108

45

THE PARADIDDLE

Singles and doubles are the two most important basic techniques for this method. Once you feel comfortable with your single and double technique, proceed to the rudiment that combines both: the paradiddle.

To develop the paradiddle to a smooth fast tempo, play the natural accent that falls on the first beat of each paradiddle. The double strokes should be bounced in order to attain maximum speed.

Exercise

Improvise in sixteenth note paradiddles around the drum set. The bass drum should be played on all 4 counts and the hi-hat on counts 2 and 4. Start the paradiddles on the snare drum. Then gradually work your way out and around all the drums of your set until you're improvising a paradiddle drum solo.

USING THE HI HAT CYMBALS

Controlling the placement of the open hi hat sound is one of the most subtle challenges of the recording studio drummer.

Here are some progressive beats that utilize the open and closed sound of the hi hat along with syncopated patterns on the bass drum.

After learning these patterns it is suggested that you continue by creating your own.

     ○ = Open sound (otherwise the hi hat cymbals remain closed; i.e. only open on the ○).

     ○ − = Open hi hat over two sixteenth notes.

(Note: when playing the open hi hat sound the preferred "open" sound is produced when the hi hat cymbals are lightly touching one another.)

Using The Hi Hat Cymbals cont....

○ = Open hi hat sound (○ – = Open hi hat sound over two sixteenth notes)

Key

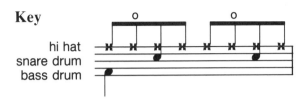

In Eighth Notes

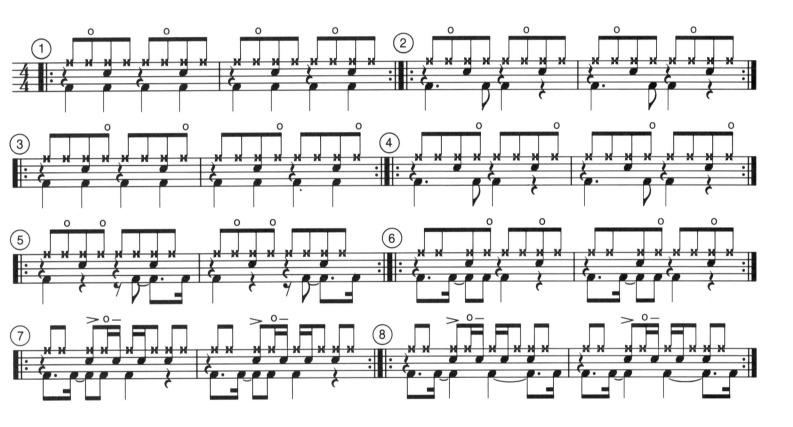

In Sixteenth Notes

Example of the sticking pattern (opposite for left handers).

Playing the hi hat with both hands in 16th notes.

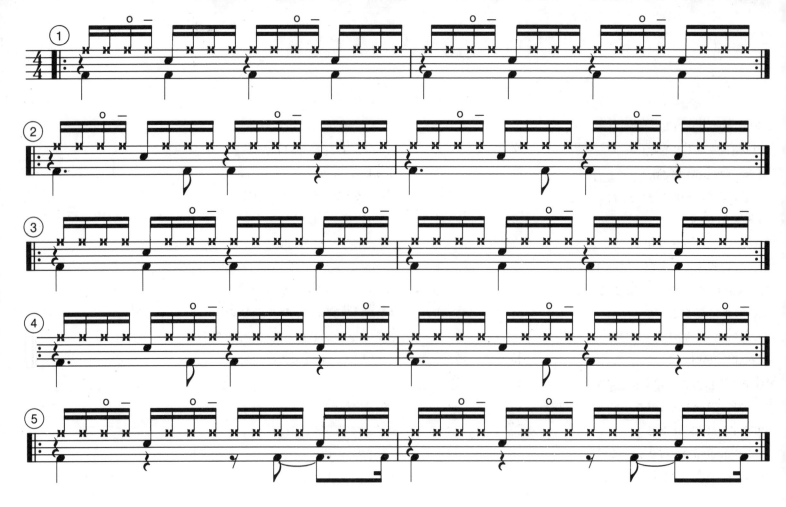

* Sticking patterns with the sixteenth notes playing through the bar.

R L R L L L R L R L R L L L R L   R L R L L L R L R L R L L L R L
  R   R   R   R

CONCLUSION

YOU HAVE JUST COMPLETED A DRUM SET BOOK DESIGNED TO TEACH YOU MANY STYLES OF DRUMMING. NOW THAT YOU **CAN** PLAY I HOPE YOU'LL GO ON TO BOOK II...A BOOK DESIGNED TO FURTHER ADVANCE YOUR DRUMMING ABILITY. LOOK FORWARD TO MORE ROCK AND JAZZ STUDIES AS WELL AS ADVANCED SOLOING, IMPROVISING, LATIN, LATIN ROCK (SALSA), JAZZ-LATIN-ROCK (FUSION), BRUSHES, READING AND MORE. SEE YOU THEN.

BEST WISHES,

Peter Magadini